DIE EMPTY

LEYONIE MARAIS

DIE EMPTY

OPERATE EACH DAY AT YOUR HIGHEST LEVEL OF GREATNESS

INSPIRED
PUBLISHING

DIE EMPTY
Operate Each Day at Your Highest Level of Greatness
First Edition, First Imprint 2024
ISBN: 978-1-7764322-2-6
Copyright © Leyonie Marais

Email the author at: leadinglady@leyoniemarais.co.za

Published by: Inspired Publishing
PO Box 82058 | Southdale | 2135 Johannesburg, South Africa
Email: info@inspiredpublishing.co.za
www.inspiredpublishing.co.za

All bible verses quoted are from the New International Version
(NIV), unless otherwise stated.

Table of Contents

Foreword

As an HR Professional, I had the desire to become an entrepreneur and joined network marketing. Learning a whole new industry, new skills, new products and ways of working was fun, exciting and really stretched me, especially the social media aspect. Continuous learning and having an open mindset have always been part of my professional guiding principles, and this "new" presented the opportunity to grow in a different way.

Following the principles of the network marketing team and reaching the leadership team, I met Leyonie Marais (Lady L). She was new to the team but quickly climbed the ladder and joined the leadership team as well. We had regular training sessions, many leader-led, and when Lady L led her first session it was clear she had a special gift. Lady L always spoke with confidence and wisdom, yet such humility. She shared key principles which helped her attain leadership status and how others could use them to build their success. She challenged us to think outside the box and really apply our minds as to how we learn, how we grow, how we succeed, leaving us in high spirits and excited about the business and opportunity. Taking ownership and accountability for your growth and success regardless of your micro and macro environmental challenges was fundamental to her teaching and not using your challenges as a crutch or permission to fail.

One of the key principles I learnt from Lady L was that your God-given gifts will make room for you and provide you with income streams. The entrepreneur in me had to tap into this source of profound wisdom and soon I had a few one-on-one sessions with Lady L to further build on my vision for my future and that of my family. These were nuggets of golden knowledge that could build my generational wealth and be a legacy left to my children to build on. A lot of the principles were faith based and that was even more relevant to me in that she was bold about her faith and bringing God into every aspect of her life, business, work, etc., never relenting on working hard while walking in God's favour.

I had the privilege of reading her book, Dethrone the Rapist, and realised what a strong, courageous, bold and beautiful woman Lady L is and that God prepared her for a time such as this. She is meant and destined to lead women and men in business and in life to be better versions of themselves. She is leading and growing leaders in different industries on various levels and spheres and always brings a fresh perspective to keep her audience engaged. Lady L has been very instrumental in my personal and professional development and I look forward to learning more from her as I continue to grow and develop in both business and life.

- **Candice February;**
Senior HR Manager & Entrepreneur

CHAPTER 1

LeadHerShip

"Success isn't something you do; success is who you become."
- Darren Hardy

As I prepared for my inaugural TV interview, a unique task loomed before me: I had to ready my children for their spotlight moment as well. The producers had expressed an interest in interviewing them, and this required a delicate conversation. I needed to explain the purpose behind the interview, outline the potential questions they might face, and brace them for inquiries from their peers once the interview had graced the national airwaves.

This task weighed heavily on me. Here I was, a mother on a mission to make a meaningful impact in the world, forced to expose my children to the often unforgiving spotlight of public scrutiny. My greatest fear was that my children might become targets of ridicule and bullying because of my story. For the first time, I had to share with them the experiences I had endured during my own childhood.

I sat down with my children and asked them a simple yet very profound question: "Tell me something about your mother." The thirteen-year-old and the seven-year-old responded with warmth and admiration. But it was the ten-year-old who caught me off guard when he said, "Mom is always angry." In that moment, I couldn't help but frown, wondering why he would utter such words on national television. And then he added, "Look, you're getting angry right now."

This hit me hard. It was a turning point for me. I got up and went to my bedroom, unable to shake off those words or the expression on his face. With tears in my eyes and a heavy heart, I wrote down my feelings in my journal. I needed to personally unpack this and understand this better because I couldn't let the world see a strong woman while my family saw a weak one.

Anger, I came to realize, was an emotion that denoted weakness — both mentally and emotionally. It was a sign of psychological fragility, and I needed to confront this truth head-on. This introspective journey led to challenging conversations, not only with my children but also with myself. If I perpetually carried this mantle of anger within the confines of my home, yet projected happiness outside its walls, there was a profound disconnect. What truly mattered to me wasn't the opinions of those who saw me in the world beyond my doorstep. What mattered most was what my children thought of me and who I was to them.

*"What does it profit a person to gain the whole world but lose their soul?" - **Mark 8:36***

My family means everything to me; they are like 'my soul'. I can't set out to change the world, fighting against abuse and rape culture, striving to bring forgiveness, hope, and healing, only to harm or lose my own family in the process. I found myself wondering if I was raising children who would need therapy because of my parenting.

This realization prompted me to take a deep look at myself, to lead myself on a path of self-discovery. This is where the concept of 'LeadHerShip' was born. I needed to understand why I was frequently angry and why my son experienced me this way. So, I had to confront this "unfavourable" truth and make it right. It meant apologizing to him and to all my children because each of them had been through this, and they might have been afraid to talk about it.

I committed to working on myself daily. I had to consciously explore the origins of my anger and why I reacted this way towards my son, and why he experienced it that way. Over the next ninety days, I challenged myself to respond differently. It wasn't easy, but I set a goal to become 1% better each day.

I had to break down the walls that prevented my children from questioning me. I had to let go of the belief that "kids are seen, not heard" and that questioning authority is disrespectful. I realized that children learn from our actions, so I needed to correct my behaviour. This meant admitting when I was wrong, acknowledging that I wasn't always right.

I encouraged them to speak their minds and made sure they felt safe doing so. This was a huge shift for me, unlearning years of parenting habits that weren't healthy. My determination was to become a better parent and provide a solid foundation for my family.

I had to learn how to manage my negative emotions and respond in a healthier way. It was like shining a spotlight on a weakness I could no longer ignore or blame on others. I had to tackle this toxic emotion before it could harm my family or, worse, become a weakness for my children.

Growing up, I was never able to express myself or find my voice. I was always on the receiving end of raised voices. It was like an invisible crutch I carried with me. Despite my determination not to be that kind of parent, I found myself becoming exactly that. I encouraged my children every day to be their best selves, but I failed to teach them how to express themselves because my responses to their questions often led to negative emotions.

Now, it was time for me to change the course of my parenting journey and pave a better path for my descendants. Just as I challenged myself years ago to be a better wife, I embarked on a journey to manage my emotions, respond differently, and ultimately become a better parent.

I Grow

I wrote in green ink on a white sheet pinned to my bedroom closet, 'I respond from a place of peace because I am in control of my emotions. I master my emotions daily.' Every morning, seeing this note served as a daily reminder to manage my emotions, thoughts, and habits. It wasn't an easy task; some days were smoother than others. But as the day drew to a close, I'd reflect on how I had responded, where I needed to make amends, and where apologies were due. My personal goal became growth, and to achieve that, I needed to learn, read, and explore. To gauge my emotional progress, I held myself accountable.

Fixed Mindset

When I think of a 'fixed mindset,' I envision a brain emoji trapped in solid cement. There's no way out unless you take a concrete hammer to it. This process can take hours or even days, depending on how eager you are to change these unhelpful behaviours. It's tempting to stick with old habits, but true liberation comes from growth and the development of healthy new habits. I had to actively address my fixed mindset.

The following characteristics are paragons to a fixed mindset:

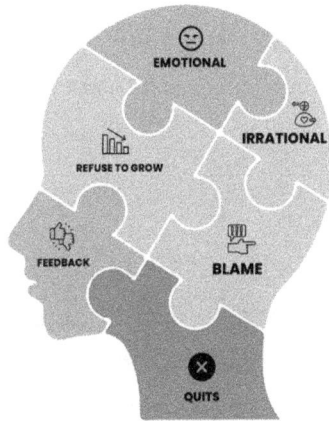

Emotional
I used to be quite emotional, often making decisions based on my emotions and reacting like an active volcano, ready to erupt at any moment.

Irrational
I acted unreasonably, frequently seeking solace in others and turning to social media when faced with problems. It dawned on me that my pursuit of unrealistic perfection was unhealthy. I had to learn how to handle conflicts within

myself, within my household, and in other areas of my life. Since charity begins at home, I decided to make my home my training ground.

Blaming Others
I had a habit of placing blame on everyone but myself. Whether it was my mother, my family, or other circumstances, I never took responsibility for where I found myself.

Resistance to Growth
My fixed mindset made it difficult for me to recognize the need for change, and it even deterred others from addressing my anger issues. I often wondered how many people had walked away from me because I was challenging to deal with and refused to acknowledge my negative patterns.

Not Open to Receiving Feedback
People with fixed mindsets tend to struggle with feedback. We tend to take all feedback personally, assuming that everyone is trying to harm us or is jealous of us.

Tendency to Quit

We tend to be quick to quit when things don't go our way. Whether it's hopping from one job to another or moving from one relationship to the next, we rarely see things through to the end because we view every challenge as a reason to give up. We always find an excuse to quit.

Growth Mindset

Imagine yourself as clay on a potter's wheel, and the potter is there, fully present, and aware of every detail. The potter knows when to apply pressure, when to add water, when to use new techniques and tools. That is what I felt like for months — a piece of clay on the potter's wheel, undergoing daily shaping. It was not easy; it required hard work, practice, and consistent effort to become better and evolve.

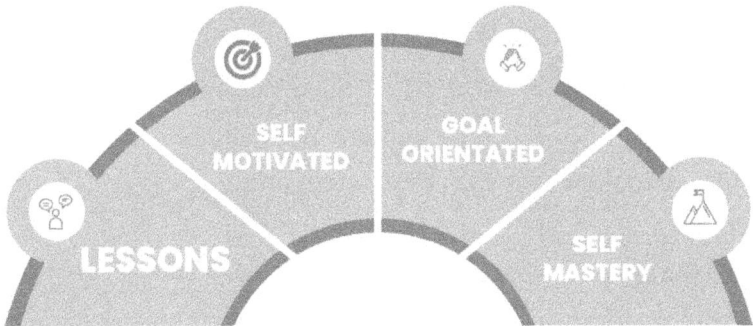

SELF MOTIVATED

GOAL ORIENTATED

LESSONS

SELF MASTERY

Lessons

I transformed every opportunity into a valuable lesson. I made it a point to identify areas where I could learn and improve. Failure became my most profound teacher, and I was determined to extract wisdom from every experience to foster my growth.

Self-Motivation

I realized waiting for external motivation from others was no longer an option. It was like a light bulb moment — I understood that no one was coming to push, motivate, or inspire me. I had to take charge of my own motivation, self-inspiration, and self-empowerment. I needed to wake up and drive myself towards improvement.

Goal Orientation

My perspective shifted from being solely goal-oriented to becoming growth-oriented. Instead of merely pursuing specific goals, I aimed to fuel my personal growth. When you focus on your growth, you naturally accomplish the goals that align with your life's vision and purpose.

Self-Mastery

I had to lead not only others but also myself — my emotions, thoughts, body, and spirit. I realized that treating myself, my husband, and my children with respect daily was essential before I could extend that respect to others. I shifted from responding with anger to responding with a sense of personal growth and inner peace. My focus transitioned from leading others to leading myself – 'LeadHerShip.'

Values

'LeadHerShip' felt like a daily routine, much like brushing my teeth. I had to continually work on myself, assessing where I was, where I wanted to be, and how I would get there. To succeed in 'LeadHerShip,' I needed to determine what held the highest value for me.

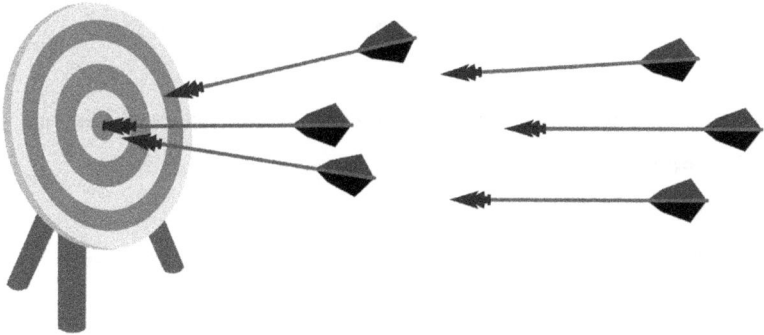

I asked myself: What occupies my thoughts the most? What do I read, eat, watch, and study? What conversations do I engage in with myself and others? What consumes my time, space, and energy? Most importantly, where do I allocate my finances? What are my primary goals, and who or what inspires me?

By answering these questions, I uncovered what held the highest value in my life. It became clear that I needed to reshape my habits, replacing the old with the new, reallocating my time wisely, and letting go of things that no longer served me. Embracing a growth mindset meant living a life guided by values; consistently and intentionally.

I recognized that a growth mindset began with my thoughts. So, I chose to focus on thoughts that were pure, kind, and positive, understanding that my thoughts would influence the passion in my heart and the outcomes in my life.

The scripture, **"As a man thinketh in his heart, so is he" - Proverbs 23:7,** was a profound paradigm shift for me. It transformed my life, leading to personal growth and increased joy. I realized that everything I have and experience is a result of my daily thoughts.

CHAPTER 2

My Success Strategy

"As you progress on your journey to success, always remember that what happens within you is more significant than what happens to you." **- John C. Maxwell**

Becoming a TEDx Speaker had been a prominent aspiration on my vision sheet. Speaking those aspirations into existence daily could not compare to the overwhelming emotions I felt on that morning when I received the invitation letter to speak at a TEDx Event. I had been diligently preparing for this moment for the past three years, both mentally and physically.

Defining Success

Let's take a moment to close our eyes and think about someone we consider successful. It could be a celebrity, a family member, or a friend. Now, you may open your eyes.

It's important to realize that we don't all measure success using the same yardstick. For some, success means luxury cars, penthouses, and multiple holiday homes. For others, it's about finding peace of mind, emotional strength, and contentment.

Now, imagine an iceberg. The person you thought of as successful when you closed your eyes is at the top of that iceberg. When you look at their life, their achievements, you're seeing the tip of the iceberg. What you do not see is the journey they took to get there — the challenges they faced, the sacrifices they made, the things they had to let go of, or what they lost along the way. You have no view of the bottom of the ocean, the unseen foundation that supports that towering iceberg.

Allow me to guide you through the steps of building that foundation, the seed to achieving great success — a strong iceberg.

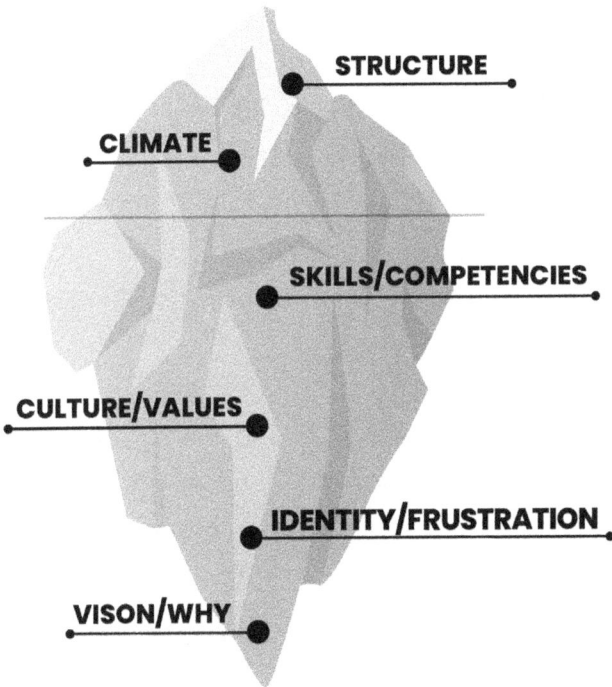

STRUCTURE

CLIMATE

SKILLS/COMPETENCIES

CULTURE/VALUES

IDENTITY/FRUSTRATION

VISON/WHY

Vision/Why

Write down your vision in a journal and also jot down why you want to achieve it. Always remember, if your vision doesn't scare you, it's not ambitious enough.

I want my vision to be a constant presence in my life, so I write it down and place it on my wall. Every morning when I wake up, it's the first thing I see, and before I sleep at night, it's the last thing I see. I read it aloud and express gratitude for my progress towards it. Every day, I work diligently to bring my vision to life, measuring my actions against my daily tasks. I ensure that my daily efforts align with this vision because any day I don't work towards it is a day wasted.

Identity/Frustration

Ask yourself, who am I? What drives me? Where do I come from? What frustrates me?

I was born and raised in Eldorado Park, in a poor family, raised by a single mother. I witnessed her relentless struggle, juggling a job and side hustles to make ends meet. I'm certain that my mom did her absolute best to ensure we never went to bed hungry. Today, as a mother of four, I'm determined not to subject my children to the same hardships I endured. I want a better life for them. However, I found myself in my mom's shoes, facing more months than money. This was my most significant frustration.

So, how did I plan to change this?

I understood that frustration could lead to either self-destruction or motivation toward greatness. I had to take steps to channel this frustration constructively. Identity and frustration are essential building blocks. Without them, your empire is incomplete and unstable.

Where do you find yourself in this scenario?

Culture/Values

We often underestimate the significance of our culture and values when building our empires. Staying rooted in your culture and values is vital for success.

Integrity is a core value I uphold. Throughout my journey to greatness and empire-building, I applied this principle to every aspect of my life. Whether it was a business opportunity, a meeting, or a signed deal, I held firm to my integrity. If a deal ever compromised my values, I walked away from it with pride. No opportunity or deal was worth jeopardizing my cultural integrity.

Here's a wake-up call: In 2017, I started cultivating produce. I had never planted habanero seeds and harvested strawberries. What you sow in the ground will eventually grow. So, when you reach the peak of your iceberg and it's time to reap the rewards, remember the seeds you planted, the sacrifices you made, and the impact on others as you climbed from the bottom of the iceberg.

As you build your empire, treat people with kindness and integrity. Don't step on others to reach the top, and don't belittle anyone to demonstrate strength or authority. If any deal or operation requires you to compromise your culture or values, walk away.

Skills/Competencies

At the tender age of nineteen, I embarked on my career as an Executive Assistant, a role I loved. I absorbed valuable skills from every executive office I managed. I leveraged these skills in building my empire, focusing on Time Management, Delegation, Organized Planning, and Recharging.

I confess, I can't count to save my life. So, when it came to calculations, I turned to Excel, a calculator, or enlisted the help of my husband. In today's world, I'd probably ask Alexa. The point is, utilize your strengths to build your empire and delegate the rest to experts. I wouldn't waste three days struggling to balance an income statement when I could hire an expert to do it, saving me precious time to work on what truly matters to me — creating content for my next talk or leadership training session.

Climate

This is where mindset plays a pivotal role. Individuals with a fixed mindset are unlikely to succeed as entrepreneurs, athletes, authors, or change-makers. A growth mindset is crucial for fostering a positive climate.

Take a moment to assess your surroundings, the people at your table. When I crafted my life plan, I had to make room for some people to leave. I also ensured that my climate allowed for me to engage in difficult conversations, both with myself and with others. It's easy to talk about toxic people, but have you ever considered if you, too, might be toxic?

I had to be honest with myself and acknowledge that I hadn't always treated everyone well. Some people I interacted with could justifiably label me as "toxic." It takes maturity to admit this. To succeed according to my life plan, I had to work on myself. Effective leadership begins with self-leadership. Changing my climate began with self-reflection, looking inward before addressing those in front of me or beside me.

27

Now, with your eyes closed, envision yourself at your grandest launch. Everything you've written on your vision sheet is becoming a reality today. Visualize the people seated in the front row, the first five, ten, or even three seats. Examine who occupies those seats. Now, open your eyes and ask yourself, "Do I want these people in my front row?"

"Practice OQP — Only Quality People," as Les Brown puts it. This means everyone in my front seats should bring quality to my table, just as I bring quality to theirs. Now, flip the script. Imagine the people in your front-row seats are launching their biggest dreams. Are you seated in their front-row seats? If not, why not? They may not see you as a quality person they need at their table.

The essence of climate lies in partnership and collaboration. This attribute is found only among successful individuals and companies.

Successful people partner with other successful people. Major banks partner, and insurance companies partner. Until you've partnered with someone, you won't reach the pinnacle of your iceberg. Seek out partners; leaders collaborate; they don't isolate.

Structure

The final pillar of my success strategy is hard work. Returning to my 2017 vision sheet, I had to break down each aspiration and create a structure to guide my path to achieving them. One of my aspirations was to launch my first book. I established daily tasks to ensure I met my deadlines, as outlined on my vision sheet. I had a deadline to deliver my manuscript to my publisher, necessitating changes to my daily habits.

No longer could I indulge in aimless social media scrolling, partying, binge-watching TV series, or participating in meaningless activities. My growth mindset had to take over and shape my daily routines, ensuring I remained focused on my vision.

High-performance individuals don't necessarily do extraordinary things; they excel at doing ordinary things extraordinarily. They are driven by their own vision and purpose, not by crowds. I often retired to bed long after my husband and children and rose before them because successful people don't adhere to the same bedtime and wake-up routines as everyone else. I wake every morning to the sound of my dreams and my vision.

Today, I lead myself to operate at my highest level of greatness each day, living a purpose-driven life daily.

CHAPTER 3

Balance

"Knowing what you need to do to improve your life takes wisdom. Pushing yourself to do it takes courage."
- Mel Robbins

I was so dedicated to being a good wife and mother that I lost sight of the fact that I was also a woman with dreams and aspirations. My husband never expected me to abandon my dreams. I looked after everyone and everything except myself. After years of nurturing my marriage and home, I began to feel that something was missing. Fearful of what people might say, I kept these feelings to myself and turned to my notebook. William Shakespeare's quote echoed in my mind: "A jack of all trades is a master of none, but oftentimes better than a master of one."

I realized I was more than just a wife and mother, and I could excel at those roles while pursuing my other aspirations. It was time to establish balance and cultivate structured, healthy habits to support my dreams and aspirations.

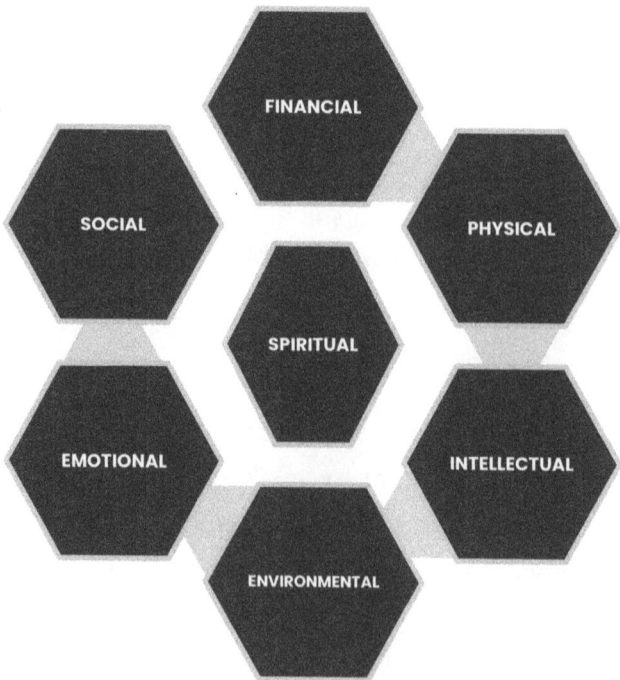

The Power of Balance

A balanced life starts with having candid conversations with oneself and being open to having these conversations with loved ones. I recognize that balance involves both vertical and horizontal relationships. To achieve equilibrium and nurture my purpose, I focus on seven key areas daily. I call it my 7 buckets. These areas serve as the pillars of my work and life balance.

Spiritual

My spiritual bucket represents my vertical relationship, my foundation. It is the core of my existence, values, and success, where I connect with my higher power, God. Whatever higher power you personally connect with. In my Christian journey, I understand this as a relationship. To strengthen my horizontal relationships, I needed to cultivate my vertical relationship.

I fortified my foundation through daily prayer, Bible study, meditation, and regular fasting. With my family, we engage in scripture reading and gratitude sessions after dinner. Additionally, I strive to treat others with respect and kindness and offer assistance to the less fortunate without seeking recognition or repayment. My family remains my top priority.

As a coach, I am excited to guide you on this journey to fortify your core existence, values, and success through your relationship with your creator. Remember, a strong foundation is essential for all your horizontal relationships to thrive. To achieve this, commit to your daily practices. Dedicate time for heartfelt prayers, Bible study, and meditation each morning. Regular fasting can also contribute to your spiritual growth. As you walk your path, embrace the significance of nurturing your relationship with your higher power. Engage your family in this beautiful journey by incorporating scripture reading and gratitude sessions daily. By doing so, you will not only strengthen your spiritual bond but also foster a harmonious home environment. In your interactions with others, always uphold respect and kindness, seeking opportunities to assist those in need without expecting praise or repayment. Above all, prioritize your family and give them your best. By remaining steadfast in these practices and continuously nurturing your vertical relationship, you will find that your horizontal relationships naturally flourish. Embrace this coaching, put it into action, and witness how your spiritual growth positively impacts all facets of your life.

Keep up the excellent work!

Physical

"Before a person can rise, conquer, and achieve, they must elevate themselves from sluggish animal indulgence."
- James Allen

This bucket has posed a challenge for me over the years. At times, healthy eating seemed costly, and finding time for exercise amid my responsibilities as a mother of four was daunting. I could always find excuses until I read James Allen's book, "As a Man Thinketh." It compelled me to reconsider my choices.

While purchasing healthy food may seem expensive now, it will undoubtedly contribute to my overall health in the long run, potentially reducing future medical expenses. So, I had to make a choice: invest in nutritious food today and enjoy a longer, healthier retirement or opt for cheaper, less healthy options and potentially incur higher medical costs when I'm older. I chose to prioritize my well-being.

I now rise at 04:50 every morning to engage in a twenty-minute run or walk around my apartment complex. On rainy days, I exercise in my living room with the aid of YouTube videos featuring Taebo, HIIT, or Pilates workouts. I kickstart my day with two glasses of water instead of coffee, ensuring I have a glass of water every hour during my working day to reach eight glasses of water per day. I follow a clean eating regimen and take my daily supplements. Taking care of my body has become a top priority.

As you embark on this journey of self-improvement and embrace a healthier lifestyle, remember the immense power of your thoughts and actions. By aligning them with your aspirations, you can achieve lasting transformation. Stay committed, maintain a positive mindset, and always believe in your ability to create the life you desire.

You've got this!

Intellectual

My vision for myself was grand, and I needed to show up daily as the person I envisioned. This required a different approach and self-improvement on all levels. I aimed to engage in meaningful, intellectual conversations in various settings, from boardrooms to social gatherings. To achieve this, I committed to growth: empowering myself and dedicating time to daily study.

In this bucket, I made a pledge to read a book every month, listen to daily podcasts, enroll in online courses every six weeks, and explore new hobbies. By turning this vision into reality, I could consistently present myself as the person I aspired to be. To accomplish this, I committed to daily self-improvement, engaging in meaningful intellectual discussions in diverse settings, from boardrooms to social events. My journey towards growth began with empowering myself. To cultivate a learning mindset, I committed to reading a book each month, listening to podcasts daily, and participating in online courses every six weeks. Cultivating new hobbies also contributed to my overall development. Stay focused and determined on this path of self-improvement, and you will unlock your true leadership potential.

Environment

"Treat others the same way you want them to treat you."
- Luke 6 v 31

This bucket serves as the compass for everything mentioned above. My Tribe, including my husband, children, family, peers, colleagues, business partners, and my team, sets the tone for my environment. How I treat others mirrors how much I invest in myself. To maintain my relationships and sustain a positive environment, I needed to measure my self-love and cultivate a culture of love, respect, empathy, and kindness for myself. I understood that I couldn't pour from an empty cup, but rather from one that overflowed into the saucer. When the saucer was empty, I couldn't replenish my environment.

By committing to progress on all levels of your being, you may realize the vision you have for yourself. By reading a book every month, listening to podcasts every day, taking online courses every six weeks, and developing new interests, you can empower yourself to have intelligent conversations in boardrooms, around dinner tables, and at social gatherings. Develop the practice of improving yourself every day to release your brilliance.

Emotional

As someone who was always prone to emotional outbursts, this bucket required significant effort and continues to do so. I had to master the art of responding differently, a skill honed through self-awareness and maturity. Learning to breathe, taking time-outs, daily journaling, and holding myself accountable for my emotional responses and interactions with others became essential. Emotional growth became the pathway to inner peace, one that extended throughout my life – within myself, my home, my workplace, and my environment. Achieving this level of growth demanded humility.

I encourage you to embark on your own journey of emotional growth. Embrace self-awareness, nurture your emotional intelligence, and commit to accountability. Through these steps, you can attain a profound sense of inner peace and foster a more harmonious and successful business environment. Remember that growth is an ongoing process, and with dedication and humility, you'll unlock new levels of success and fulfillment.

Social

"As iron sharpens iron, so will one person be to another."
- Proverbs 27 v 17

I shifted my prayer from asking God to remove fake people from my life to a different plea – that I may grow into a quality person. A person who sharpens others, leaving them better than I found them. As I evolved into a quality individual, my focus naturally changed, and so did my circle. Front-row seats were now reserved for like-minded people who operated at their highest level of greatness, attracting greatness in return.

I transitioned from a scarcity mindset to an abundance mindset. Picking up my phone in the morning and mindlessly scrolling through social media was no longer an option; it had become a distraction to my pursuit of greatness. I turned off the noise of news feeds and turned on the wisdom of mind feeds – strong individuals who dedicated their lives to greatness.

I immersed myself in circles where conversations centered on success, significance, and purpose. But the next level of my life unfolded when I encountered three powerful words: Coach, Mentor, and Sponsor.

A Coach engages with you, providing guidance and developmental tools. A Mentor walks with you, aiding in navigating tough career decisions. Sponsors speak about you in places and spaces where you might not have access, influencing your growth and advancement.

This challenge felt bigger than me. Was I prepared to hear about my flaws and weaknesses, be transparent about where I wanted to go, and remain open to learning, applying, and growing?

Feedback had always triggered negative emotions in me; I couldn't handle it. I viewed it as a weapon of destruction. But now, having grown into a more complete individual, I was eager to embark on this journey.

Today, I have a coach, mentor, and sponsor for each of my talents. These remarkable individuals serve as key gate-keepers in my life and trusted sounding boards. My success bears the fruits of their labour. I had learned that those serious about achieving success always have a coach. Every high-performing athlete has one, and so should I.

As you continue on this path of personal growth, remember to stay aligned with your purpose and remain receptive to new opportunities and challenges. Keep seeking knowledge, surround yourself with mentors, coaches, and sponsors, and never shy away from reaching for even greater heights. Your commitment to personal development will undoubtedly lead you to a fulfilling and impactful life.

Keep shining and inspiring others on their own journeys to greatness!

Financial
Living hand to mouth was no longer an acceptable option. I recognized the need to gain control over my finances. It had become a recurring cycle to borrow money every month just to scrape through the last few days of it, and it felt like a never-ending curse. Financial literacy became my lifeline.

My journey began by establishing a budget and, most importantly, adhering to it. The next crucial step was to embrace a lifestyle that aligned with my financial means. I ceased purchasing items I didn't genuinely need.

Breaking free from the shackles of living paycheck to paycheck and escaping the relentless rat race of generational poverty and financial stagnation became my paramount aspiration. My newfound strategy focused on living within my financial means while creating a legacy for my descendants. Seventy percent of my income was allocated to cover living expenses, 10% was dedicated to giving back, 10% for investments, and the remaining 10% was reserved as a reward for myself. If I couldn't sustain my life within that 70%, it meant I was living beyond my financial means.

In this financial realm, I adopted the philosophy of LEARN-EARN-GIVE-EAT.

The power of balance lies in the unwavering commitment to these seven buckets. It elevated my purpose, inspiring not only myself but unlocking my higher calling to assist others. This, in essence, is my legacy, propelling me into the next dimension of my greatness.

Having a newfound purpose allows you to rewrite your legacy, open doors to financial independence and wealth, construct a brighter future, and leave an indelible mark on your descendants. You have the power to guide your children toward financial freedom and personal fulfillment by sharing this invaluable knowledge with them.

CHAPTER 4

Discover Your
Greatness

"You want to make sure that your purpose is something people benefit from long after you've gone." **- Bob Proctor**

The question, "Leyonie, how does your husband feel about your success?" has been posed to me countless times. Initially, I couldn't grasp why this question seemed to stir up conversations repeatedly. I decided to delve deeper and investigate.

I eventually arrived at an understanding that due to our cultural differences, successful women were often met with disapproval and sometimes even considered volatile. Traditional values had perpetuated the notion that a woman's place was in the kitchen, surrounded by her children. Being a good mother and wife was the ideal upheld by our grandparents and their ancestors. However, times have evolved, and a woman's role is no longer solely defined by her marital or parental status.

Many women find themselves dimming their own aspirations, careers, growth and plans to accommodate their partners, sometimes at the expense of their own dreams. Perhaps they had no dreams before the relationship, or if they did, those dreams suddenly lost their value. But there are also women, like myself, who choose to temporarily set aside their ambitions to establish a strong foundation at home, to build structure and tone.

My consistent response to this question has always remained unchanged: my husband wholeheartedly supports my success, celebrates my achievements, and takes pride in my accomplishments.

A man who knows his worth will never hinder his partner's brilliance; instead, he will inspire her to shine, finding pride in her success, recognizing that her achievements only enhance their shared success. My husband and I do not see each other as competitors; we are partners who complement, uplift, and celebrate each other. When circumstances require us to adapt our roles for the harmonious functioning of our home, we do so with love and cooperation.

Furthermore, I've come to understand that my success is rooted in being a balanced, multi-talented woman. I am an individual before I am a wife, mother, or daughter; I am so much more. I have been crafted with a unique blueprint, a purpose, and I am obligated to fulfill that purpose. This responsibility extends to both myself and my creator, as I owe it to us both to live life to the fullest. I refuse to leave this world with my gifts and talents buried within me; my aim is to depart empty, having lived a purpose-driven life and shared all of my gifts and talents.

I, Leyonie Marais, dedicate each day to operating at my highest level of greatness. I relentlessly pursue all my gifts and talents daily.

Power to Create Wealth

"According to the abilities of each man, one servant received five talents, the second received two, and the third received only one."
- Matthew 25 v 14

I'd like to draw your attention to this parable. A master went away and entrusted each of his servants with talents. Upon his return, he inquired about what they had done with these talents. Two of the three servants multiplied their talents, but the third chose to bury his one talent, keeping it safe for the master's return.

Upon researching this parable and the significance of talents, I learned that one talent was equivalent to twenty years of labour and weighed about seventy-five pounds in gold or silver. In simpler terms, your talents should sustain you throughout your retirement and serve as a heritage for your children.

I made a commitment to myself: I refuse to depart this world with my potential untapped. I refuse to die full; I will die empty. I diligently worked on myself every day, much like tending to a garden. I showed up for myself, punctual and present. This journey of self-improvement led me to discover my worth, my talents, and ultimately, myself. I uncovered my first talent, which gave birth to a second, and I honed these talents, sharpening my skills. The more I invested in myself, the more talents I unearthed. Each talent acted as a seed for the next one, forming a strong foundation as illustrated below. My talent scale grew exponentially, with T1 spilling into T2, T2 into T3, and ultimately becoming a wellspring of wealth for both myself and my household. Being multi-talented equated to multiple streams of income, perpetually flowing. Every morning I wake up, I express gratitude to God for the talents that empower me to create wealth.

This revelation arrived during the heart of the Covid-19 pandemic, following a period of devastating loss. I was left pondering how to provide for our children, and in response, God's message resonated: "Your gifts will make room for you and place you before great men" - **Proverbs 18 v 16.** "I have given you the power to create wealth" - **Deuteronomy 8 v 18.**

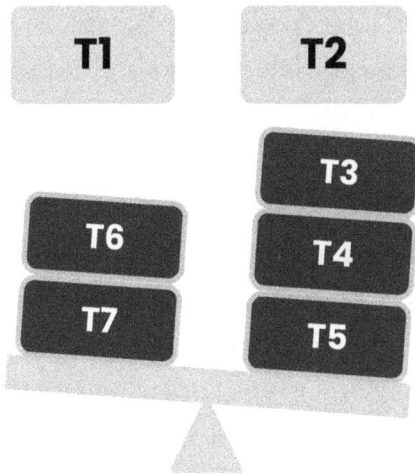

My Greatness at Work

My professional journey began at the age of nineteen as an Executive Assistant. I never stayed with a single company for more than three years and never celebrated a long-service award. I was often labeled a 'job hopper.' My career as an Executive Assistant taught me valuable skills in serving, prioritizing, delegating, and managing executives. I excelled in this role, winning numerous awards and being likened to the 'Donna Paulsen' of my time. However, every three years, I found myself at a crossroads — drained, frustrated, and ready to move on. Sunday evenings were particularly daunting as I contemplated the upcoming workweek, wondering how much longer I could endure.

Sometimes I left jobs due to toxic bosses, and other times it was simply because I felt drained and frustrated. This had become my norm.

However, in 2017, I started a Non-Profit Organization (NPO), and during weekends, I experienced a profound transformation. I began to operate at my highest level of greatness, empowering others and guiding them towards their own greatness. On weekdays, it was a different story; I felt frustrated, stagnant, and unfulfilled for years. But on weekends, I came alive when operating within my greatness. This perplexed me, and I embarked on a journey of introspection, examining not only my own career but also that of my mother and other loved ones.

My mother had retired early in her forties, citing exhaustion and a need for rest after working since the age of sixteen. Ironically, two years later, she returned to a nine-to-five job, but this time in a different role. Prior to retirement, she worked as a creditors clerk, but upon her return, she was in a role that allowed her to serve others. The crucial difference was that she was now operating at her highest level of greatness, and she thrived. This led me to realize that her exhaustion wasn't solely due to her role but because she had not been operating at her fullest potential.

Two years later, she stepped into a role that allowed her to do just that, and at the age of sixty-four, she continues to serve others with enthusiasm.

In my case, I had a pattern of resigning every three years due to exhaustion. Despite being skilled at my job, it drained me because, like my mother, I wasn't operating at my highest level of greatness. Now, in my forties, I was appointed to a voluntary serving role where I could finally operate at my highest level of greatness, leading to a career change that allowed me to live a purpose-driven life by operating within my greatness.

It's worth noting that my CV had the title of Executive Assistant for decades, and I was often pigeonholed into this role due to my experience. However, what I needed wasn't a new job but a career change that would shift me from operating out of frustration to my highest level of greatness.

As a leader and an entrepreneur I have two fundamental principles when hiring:

1. I prioritize understanding what candidates excel at rather than focusing solely on their experience.

2. I aim to assemble the right team, remove individuals who don't fit, and ensure the right people are in the right roles while investing in their development.

Bottom Line

Your values lead to your purpose, which, in turn, gives birth to your legacy. For me, the bottom line is about discovering my greatness, pursuing it daily, and creating a legacy characterized by substance, wealth, and peace.

Identifying my greatness has defined my purpose, and helping others discover their greatness has become my higher purpose.

CHAPTER 5

Mind Your Business

"The growth and development of people is the highest calling of leadership." - **Harvey Firestone**

Entrepreneurship

In this chapter, I want to distinguish between a mere businessman or woman and an entrepreneur. You see, a businessman operates with an existing idea, but an entrepreneur? Well, an entrepreneur is someone who carries a new idea that has the power to bring about change. Think of it this way: a businessman sells lemons, while an entrepreneur takes those lemons and turns them into refreshing lemonade.

"God didn't create desks and chairs He created trees."
- Bishop TD Jakes

One thing I'm passionate about is supporting my community's entrepreneurs. I celebrate their endeavours and extend my support wholeheartedly. As an entrepreneur myself, I treat every fellow entrepreneur with the same respect and support that I hope to receive. Sadly, not everyone in our entrepreneurial community operates with this level of respect.

I hold my craft in high regard, and that extends to my clients. When I take on a project, I make sure to request a detailed brief from my clients, ensuring that I can deliver precisely what they need. There's no room for subpar service in my approach. I'm committed to being punctual and well-prepared, which is why I never overcommit myself to multiple engagements in a single day. I firmly believe that every event is an opportunity to make a profound impact on my audience, and that impact ripples through their lives, homes, communities, and organizations.

When I accept a speaking engagement or a corporate training session, I always arrive at my highest level of greatness. I hold deep respect for myself, my talents, and my clients. Whether it's a big or small invoice, I treat every client with the utmost respect because I understand the significance of speaking into people's lives. I'm fully aware that my talent will pave the way for me and position me among great individuals. However, I'm not naive enough to think that I'm irreplaceable. To me, underserving opportunities are akin to burying my own talent.

Minding my business means approaching my customers with respect and empathy.

80/20 Rule

I visualize my business as a ship. Everyone on board has their task, passion, talents, and gifts. My role is to steer the ship in the right direction. Over the years, I've attended countless workshops, seminars, and leadership training sessions.

But a crucial question arose: "How much training do I need before I start putting my knowledge into action?" Knowledge alone isn't power; it's the application of that knowledge that truly empowers.

It dawned on me that to be a great leader, I had to lead myself first. I experienced a significant growth spurt when I realized that leadership is 80% leading myself and only 20% allowing others to lead themselves. This is the DNA of a great leader. It involves calling myself out, engaging in introspective conversations, and, most importantly, being open to feedback. I've learned to listen to understand, rather than simply listening to respond.

A leader who can motivate themselves to take action is a great leader indeed. To lead others effectively, I must lead myself effectively first. You cannot lead others and expect them to show up 100% if you're not leading yourself effectively.

My ultimate purpose as a leader is to help others discover their greatness and allow them to lead themselves. This is the pathway to greatness. I understand that keeping my higher purpose at the forefront of my decision-making process serves as a compass to steer my business towards greatness.

Continuous development of my leadership skills and unwavering commitment to my principles inspire my team and create a positive work environment. Leadership is an ongoing journey of growth, and with the right mindset and actions, I'm poised to continue evolving as a great leader.

Leading with Purpose

As I continue to delve into what makes a great leader, I want to emphasize that a great leader doesn't have to be an expert in every field or possess all-encompassing knowledge and skills. Instead, a truly successful leader is someone who surrounds themselves with individuals who excel in areas where they may lack expertise. This collaborative approach is a key ingredient in leadership success.

Let's explore some essential aspects of effective leadership:

- **Be Mindful**

Mindful leadership begins with the art of listening to understand, rather than merely responding. It's about recognizing that every member of your team brings a unique set of skills, temperaments and talents to the table. The key to reaching our destination on this ship is how we guide our team members to deliver their best and flourish daily.

- **Empathy**

Leading with empathy is one of the most potent leadership qualities. It attracts the best people and cultivates the most productive teams. Imagine working for a leader who demands your presence at work while your child is sick in the hospital. In such a situation, that team member would likely update their resume and start searching for a new job immediately. A true leader shows up for their people, acknowledging their personal challenges and will offer support.

- **Culture**

I once found myself in the reception area of a large company while waiting for a job interview. What caught my eye was an anonymous suggestion box. Without hesitation, I got up and walked out. You see, this signaled to me that I wouldn't be a cultural fit. An organization with an anonymous suggestion box often indicates a closed-door policy, a lack of willingness to receive feedback, and an environment where opinions must be hidden. Unfortunately, this can lead to discrimination against those who do speak up and result in retaliation. In simpler terms, it signifies a toxic work culture.

- **Have Difficult Conversations**

Great leaders are open to difficult conversations, both about themselves and their team members. They don't leave their team feeling belittled or attacked, regardless of the situation. Instead, they address issues with empathy and a focus on growth and improvement.

- **Inspire to Improve**

Leaders inspire their people to reach higher, be better, and do better. The journey from effectiveness to greatness is paved with inspiration, which in turn leads to development and growth.

- **Connect/Communicate**

Managers with a closed-door policy struggle to connect, engage, and communicate effectively. They often resort to sending generic communications. In contrast, a leader maintains an open door, fostering transparency and effortless communication. A great leader understands the power of three-way communication: Leader to Individual (L2I), Leader to Group (L2G), and Leader to Leader (L2L). These channels aren't solely for giving directives; they serve as avenues to check in, inspire, and facilitate development.

Now, let's ponder this: What's the first step you'll take as a leader to create a workplace culture where ideas flow freely, and collaboration thrives? How can you shift the focus from mere numbers to the individuals who make up your team? Creating a psychologically safe and encouraging environment where people feel inspired to realize their full potential is the hallmark of effective leadership.

Strategic Thinking

As leaders, it's crucial to declutter our minds from distractions, allowing us the time and mental space to think, evaluate, and plan. I encourage you to set aside dedicated periods quarterly and annually, away from the office and family commitments, for strategic reflection and planning. During these times, craft a strategic plan with clear objectives.

One of the most pressing challenges in today's workplace is its multi-generational nature. A strong leader possesses the strategic thinking skills needed to bridge these generational gaps effectively. Encourage everyone to bring their unique assets to the boardroom or team and work on developing them for the benefit of the organization. Instead of impatience, foster a culture of mutual learning.

I implore you, fellow leaders, to prioritize strategic thinking, planning, and assessment. By taking these quarterly and annual breaks and crafting well-defined strategic plans, we can address the intricacies of a multi-generational workforce and harness the diversity of strengths it offers. Let's replace impatience with a commitment to learning from one another. With wisdom, empathy, and foresight, we can lead our organizations to flourish in an ever-evolving business landscape. By empowering our teams, embracing diversity, and nurturing a collaborative spirit, we can pave the way for unparalleled achievements.

Effectiveness to Greatness

In my quest to be a servant leader, I have embraced the principle of never being too busy for my team, always ready to lend a hand and guide them. As a servant leader, I've posed these essential questions to myself and my team members:

1. How can I help?
2. What are your core values, and what do you value most?
3. What are your strengths, and how can I support you in leveraging them?
4. What ignites your passion and inspires you?
5. What are your short-term and long-term visions for one year, three years, and five years?
6. How do you strategize during detours, seeking to emerge stronger rather than faster? Remember that pivotal lessons are often learned during these detours, so rushing through them is not advisable.
7. Define integrity. As Warren Buffet wisely noted, "when evaluating people, look for intelligence, energy, and integrity, with integrity being the most crucial."

While management entails overseeing your team, leadership involves guiding them. If your aspiration is to be a servant leader, your commitment lies in aiding your team members, acknowledging their core values and strengths, and setting a commendable example. By asking these pertinent questions, you demonstrate a genuine interest in their well-being and professional growth. Viewing detours as opportunities for learning and promoting integrity within the team solidify your role as an authentic servant leader.

Remember that leading by example and fostering open communication are pivotal in this journey. Your dedication to empowering your team and celebrating their accomplishments will establish a positive and supportive work environment, nurturing a culture of growth and success. Continue refining your leadership abilities, seeking feedback, and prioritizing a healthy work-life balance. In doing so, you will unquestionably evolve into an exceptional servant leader, inspiring and motivating your team to reach new heights.

My Business vs. Others' Business

I've adopted a simple yet profound approach to life: I mind my business. Equally important, I extend the courtesy of allowing others the space to mind their own business—embracing their thoughts, emotions, and the way they choose to treat me.

Finally, there's God's Business: my family's safety, our next meal, our health, our success, and the arrival of new opportunities. By focusing solely on these aspects, I have bid farewell to sleepless nights, finding peace in minding my own business.

As your dedicated growth coach, I encourage you to integrate these three pillars into your daily life. Embrace the transformative power of concentrating on your personal development, while liberating others to be authentic, and placing trust in the grand design of the universe. This approach will set you on a profound journey of self-discovery, fulfillment, and ultimately, an extraordinary life worth cherishing.

Remember, dear friends, the choice is yours. Embrace the philosophy of minding your business, granting space to others, and trusting in a higher power.

Welcome to a life of growth, purpose, and boundless possibilities. Together, let's embark on this transformative journey, providing support and empowerment every step of the way.

CHAPTER 6

Prepare for Where You're Going

Reinvent Yourself

In 2017, I embarked on a journey to establish my Non-Profit Organization (NPO), starting from the ground up. I meticulously ensured legal compliance and kept myself updated on the relevant legislation. My unwavering passion was to serve women and children in need. I had an abundance of ideas to rebuild my community, and I tirelessly approached corporates, churches, and individuals who, despite being rejected repeatedly, shared my vision. I organized annual fundraisers and events to sponsor safe houses and support vulnerable women. However, as time passed, I couldn't sustain funding these safe houses from my personal income, and my family bore the brunt of this decision. My frustration mounted as I couldn't fathom why corporates continued to reject us. I had been diligently serving the community — surely, they could see it. After five years of relentless rejection, persistent funding proposals, corporate pitches, and fundraising events, it was time for me to realign my approach.

I made a conscious decision to reinvent myself, rebrand, and adjust my objectives. Instead of focusing on funding safe houses, I shifted my attention to empowering women to a point where they could sustain themselves. The overarching vision remained the same, but my objective evolved — from providing immediate relief to women to empowering them for self-sufficiency. This change represented a more potent and enduring solution. Now, rather than relying on food parcels or rent assistance, these women could earn a living through the skills and services I could provide.

Adapting to the changing times, I created new tools to realize my vision, mission, and values. I was now in alignment with my organization's core values: to empower and liberate broken women, guiding them toward the next phase of their lives. My skills and knowledge became instrumental in educating and uplifting them. All it took was my willingness to reinvent myself and establish a powerful brand.

"For a just man falleth seven times, and riseth up again"
- Proverbs 24 v 16

As a visionary entrepreneur, I encountered numerous low moments, doubting whether this vision and plan were worth pursuing. But every time I looked at my bedroom wall, where my life plan hung, I realized how far I had come and how much more I could achieve. I simply needed to get up after each fall and try again. Eventually, I wasn't just trying; I was doing it, and doing it well. Remaining down was never an option because my true strength was in getting up.

You too will discover that resilience and the ability to rise above setbacks are not only empowering but also liberating. Through this transformational journey, you will access this inner strength, surmount challenges, and turn setbacks into invaluable learning experiences that propel you toward your full potential. Begin your transformational journey today, where success isn't just an attempt but a resounding achievement!

Growth Plan

- **Accountability Partner:**

Lifelong learning became my guiding principle. I transformed every situation into a learning experience. It was crystal clear that my journey to achieve, pursue, and maintain greatness demanded daily growth. I adopted a holistic approach to taking care of myself — mind, body, and spirit. This involved being mindful of what I consumed, both in terms of food and information. Equally important was my choice of companions, as I realized that the company I kept profoundly influenced my growth. Sometimes, this meant letting go of people, even if they were family. We often pray for peace, yet sometimes, we unknowingly bring storms and turmoil to those around us. Growing daily translated to glowing daily, both inwardly and outwardly. If you need to walk away from certain situations or relationships, do so without guilt.

Accountability played a pivotal role in my growth plan. Every night at 10 pm, I engaged in an accountability session. During this time, I reflected on the day, recorded what I ate, drank, and spent money on, and noted the nature of my conversations — whether they were stimulating or not. Each day, I held myself accountable for showing up for myself. After all, if I couldn't be accountable to myself, how could I be for others? It took a mere ninety days to transform myself into a self-sustaining, healthy, and accountable partner for my own life and purpose.

- **Empower Hour:**

The first hour of the day, which I termed the "empower hour," was critical in setting the tone for the rest of my day. I transformed my mornings into glorious sessions by removing all distractions from my bedroom, designating it a no-screen, no-phone zone. I purged my phone of news applications and uninstalled distracting social media platforms like Twitter and Facebook. Instead, I began my day with a sacred routine — prayer, meditation, reading, exercise, and nurturing creativity. I prioritized mind enrichment over news consumption. During the subsequent hour, I connected with my husband and children, ensuring they were ready for work and school, and I checked in with my mom and siblings. Astonishingly, I could go until 11 am without checking my phone, signifying that my previous addiction no longer obstructed my creativity or pursuit of greatness. I nourished my creativity, allowing it to give birth to my greatness during these foundational three hours of my day.

- **Affirmations:**

The power of affirmations became evident in my life transformation. Initially, my affirmations were a recitation of my fears and weaknesses, reflecting my anger, financial struggles, and paranoia.

However, in 2021, I embraced the habit of studying, and this is where I unearthed the potency of the subconscious mind. Consequently, I rewrote my affirmations and those of my children, purging them of negativity and replacing it with positivity. Understanding that the subconscious mind feeds on our thoughts, which in turn become our words, I recited and meditated upon positive affirmations. This transformation yielded profound results.

71

Rather than saying, "I do not respond from a place of anger," I affirmed, "I respond from a place of peace and growth." Instead of declaring, "I no longer live from hand to mouth," I asserted, "I live a life of abundance and overflow, reflecting in my finances and relationships."

Substituting the phrase, "keep us free from all hurt, harm, terror, and danger," with "protect my family and friends" demonstrated a profound shift.

Instead of proclaiming, "I will not give up, I will not quit," I declared, "I attract success, successful people, and successful companies because I am successful."

This newfound understanding empowered me, as I realized that through Christ, I can accomplish anything. Everything good and perfect flows into my life from God, and this divine strength and perfection reside within me, as per Ephesians 3 v 20. This strength and perfection propelled me daily.

I practiced all eight habits of highly effective people daily, emphasizing proactivity, vision, prioritization, win-win solutions, empathetic communication, synergy, self-renewal, and the journey from effectiveness to greatness. My daily routine involved harnessing the power of imagination, specialized knowledge, organized planning, and decision-making. Desiring success, maintaining faith, practicing auto-suggestion, consistency, persistence, harnessing the power of the mastermind, understanding the subconscious mind, and optimizing my brain and sixth sense all played integral roles in my daily habits.

Now that I understand what God can do through me, for me, and within me, I am fully aware that I can accomplish anything, attracting everything I desire and need. The key is applying this knowledge, for applied knowledge is power.

- **Gratitude Journal:**

The Gratitude Journal was a transformative practice in my daily routine. I want to stress just how impactful it can be. Those first five minutes in the morning and the last five minutes before sleep were sacred moments devoted to this practice. During these times, I intentionally reflected on my life and noted at least three things I was grateful for each morning and evening.

This seemingly simple act of gratitude journaling wielded profound results. By acknowledging the blessings, both big and small, that graced my life, I found myself becoming more attuned to the positive aspects of each day. This practice had a profound impact on my overall mindset and outlook.

You see, a heart filled with gratitude serves as fertile soil for the growth of blessings. It's not merely a matter of counting one's blessings but also of cultivating an attitude of appreciation. As I consistently expressed gratitude for the things I had, I began to notice even more things to be grateful for. It was as if this practice opened my eyes to the abundance surrounding me.

This practice also had a ripple effect on my interactions with others. Expressing gratitude made me more aware of the kindness and generosity of those around me. Consequently, I was more inclined to express my appreciation to others, strengthening my relationships and fostering a positive environment.

So, if you haven't already, consider incorporating a Gratitude Journal into your daily routine. Take those precious moments in the morning and evening to reflect on the blessings in your life. You'll be amazed at how this simple practice can cultivate a mindset of abundance and attract more positivity into your life.

- **Mentorship:**

Mentorship is a cornerstone of personal and professional growth, and it's something I deeply value. I believe that every successful athlete, entrepreneur, or leader can point to a mentor who played a pivotal role in their journey. Just think about it.

Warren Buffet had Benjamin Graham; Robert Kiyosaki had his rich dad; Les Brown had Zig Ziglar; and Napoleon Hill had the guidance of Andrew Carnegie. These mentors provided valuable insights, guidance, and wisdom that accelerated the growth and success of these individuals.

Now, I encourage you to ask yourself: Who is your mentor? Do you have someone in your life who can provide you with guidance, support, and perspective? Mentorship is not limited to formal relationships; it can come in various forms. It might be a trusted colleague, a seasoned professional in your field, or even someone you admire from afar.

Having a mentor can offer numerous benefits. They can help you navigate challenges, avoid common pitfalls, and provide you with insights that can be game-changing in your journey. A mentor can also serve as a source of motivation and accountability, pushing you to strive for greatness.

If you haven't already, consider seeking out a mentor who aligns with your aspirations and values. Reach out to them, build a relationship, and be open to learning from their experiences. Mentorship can be a transformative force in your personal and professional development, helping you unlock your full potential and achieve greatness.

Your Finest Hour

Winston Churchill once aptly stated, "There comes a special moment in everyone's life, a moment for which that person was born. That special opportunity, when he seizes it, will fulfill his mission — a mission for which he is uniquely qualified. At that moment, he will find greatness. It is his finest hour."

These words are profound and hold a universal truth that transcends time. They remind us that each of us has a unique path, a purpose waiting to be fulfilled, and moments where we can shine the brightest.

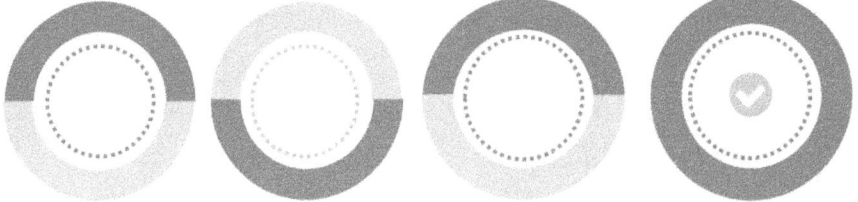

In my journey, a pivotal moment arrived a few years ago when a dear friend offered to design a website and speaker profile for me. She requested that I provide the content to add to the profile and website. Filled with enthusiasm, I hastily started the project, sending her everything I had within a day. However, her response was unexpected and thought-provoking. She called and straightforwardly stated, "My friend, you are not taking yourself seriously. What you've sent won't convince anyone to book you. You need to put more thought and effort into this."

Initially, I was taken aback and unsure of how to proceed. Marketing was her expertise, and she directed me to explore the websites of famous speakers in South Africa, urging me to model their approach. As I delved into their profiles, I was shocked by the level of professionalism and self-assuredness that emanated from their content. It made me realize that I had been underestimating the power of presenting myself authentically and confidently.

I grappled with the idea of describing myself in ways that seemed boastful. It felt as though I was thinking too much about myself. However, my friend's advice lingered in my mind: "If you want others to take you seriously, you have to take yourself seriously."

This conversation led to a significant paradigm shift in my perspective. I understood that I needed a comprehensive plan to progress. I formulated a five-year plan, setting out to work diligently on myself as a speaker and create valuable content for a website. Initially, it seemed daunting and almost impossible. I felt overwhelmed just writing them down. To make them more manageable, I developed a three-year plan and an annual plan, all of which I prominently displayed on my bedroom wall.

However, it wasn't until I incorporated daily tasks into my routine that I realized the path to achieving these long-term objectives. These daily habits became the building blocks for my annual plan, which in turn was instrumental in reaching my three-year plan. Before I knew it, I had achieved my five-year plan within three years and surpassed my three-year plan in just two years.

The profound lesson here is that we must prepare ourselves diligently for our finest hour, our most significant dreams, and our life's most pivotal moments. Each one of us has unique aspirations, and careful planning is the key to their realization. Identify a clear path that leads to your long-term objectives, and break it down into milestones, like a five-year plan divided into three-year segments. Celebrate your achievements along the way, and diligently track your progress. It's astonishing how swiftly your five-year plan can become a reality in just three years, and your three-year plan can materialize in a single year when your objectives are crystal clear and you approach your journey with unwavering positivity.

So, I urge you to prepare meticulously for where you are going. As Winston Churchill emphasized, when that special moment arrives, you won't be unprepared or squander your greatest dreams. Your journey will be a testament to your determination, drive, and the clarity of your plans. It's not merely about arriving at your finest hour but being ready to embrace it fully when it comes.

Self-Destruct

As you contemplate scaling the next hill in your life's journey, I implore you to approach it with a mindful strategy. Resist the temptation to launch into it at the same frenetic pace you maintained during your previous ascent. It's crucial to understand that this new challenge requires a different approach. Take a moment to slow down, and if necessary, walk a few steps. This brief pause allows you to realign your thoughts and regain control of your breathing.
The truth is, the pace at which you ascend the hill is not the most formidable obstacle you'll encounter; it's your mindset and your ability to regulate your breath that will determine your success. As you approach the final stretch of your race, remember that finishing strong is not just an option; it's a requirement. Summon all your reserves of energy and determination, and make a decisive push towards the finish line.

The overarching principle to guide you is to continually operate at your highest level of greatness. Embrace the idea of multiplying your talents and ensuring you leave this world with an empty well of potential. When your finest hour eventually arrives, may it find you fully prepared, both in your mindset and your physical readiness.

In summary, the key to your ongoing success and personal evolution lies in your ability to adapt to the changing terrain of life's journey. Don't let past achievements set an unrealistic pace for your future endeavours. Instead, approach each new challenge with mindfulness, acknowledging that your mindset and breath control are the true determinants of your outcome. Keep your focus on finishing strong, and strive to operate at the highest level of your greatness in everything you do. As you multiply your talents and make the most of every opportunity, rest assured that when your finest hour arrives, you will be more than ready to embrace it with open arms.

Do not be that servant who buried his talent. Multiply your talent, empower your community, define your legacy so you may, DIE EMPTY.

About the Author

Leyonie Marais is a devoted wife and mother of four, embodying the essence of family values in her everyday life. Beyond her roles within the home, she emerges as a compelling figure on the public stage — a TEDx speaker and activist.

In her work, Leyonie paints a vivid picture of a world where the privileged and underprivileged coexist, standing shoulder to shoulder, and fostering an environment where mutual learning leads to positive change. Her ability to bridge divides and create unity in diversity shines through in both her writing and public engagements.

Leyonie's influence extends beyond the written word, as evidenced by the acclaim received for her previous book and Masterclasses, she is recognized for her unparalleled skills in navigating and 'Leading Difficult Conversations'. Respected by leaders and organizations within her sphere of operation, Leyonie has become a beacon of inspiration for those seeking to make a meaningful impact on their environment.

With a clear mandate to impact the world one person at a time, Leyonie Marais is on a mission to create positive ripples of change. To learn more about her work and insights, visit www.leyoniemarais.co.za. As an author, speaker, and coach, Leyonie invites you to join her in shaping a world where compassion and understanding guide the path to a brighter future.